W9-BII-779

DATE DUE

Ancient Myths
The Twelve Labors
of Hercules

Written by
James Ford

Illustrated by
Peter Rutherford

Created and designed by
David Salariya

PICTURE WINDOW BOOKS
Minneapolis, Minnesota

First published in the United States in 2005
by Picture Window Books
5115 Excelsior Boulevard
Minneapolis, MN 55416
1-877-845-8392
www.picturewindowbooks.com

First published in Great Britain in 2004 by Book House,
an imprint of The Salariya Book Company, Ltd.,
25 Marlborough Place, Brighton BN1 1UB
Please visit The Salariya Book Company at
www.salariya.com or *www.book-house.co.uk*

Library of Congress Cataloging-in-Publication Data
Ford, James Evelyn.
The twelve labors of Hercules / by James Ford ; illustrated by
Peter Rutherford.
    p. cm. — (Ancient myths)
Includes index.
ISBN 1-4048-0904-X (hardcover)
1. Heracles (Greek mythology)—Juvenile literature.
2. Hercules (Roman mythology)—Juvenile literature.
I. Rutherford, Peter. II. Title. III. Series.
BL820.H5F67 2004
398.2'0938'02—dc22   2004007368

Content Adviser: Professor William D. Dyer, Humanities Director,
English Department, Minnesota State University, Mankato

Editors: Michael Ford, Nadia Higgins

About the Author: James Ford studied English and Classics at
Oxford University. He taught English in Greece before returning
to England to work in publishing.

About the Illustrator: Peter Rutherford lives and works in
Suffolk, England, and has been illustrating children's books for
the past 10 years.

About the Series Creator: David Salariya was born in Dundee,
Scotland. He has illustrated a wide range of books and has
created and designed many new series for publishers worldwide.
In 1989, he established The Salariya Book Company. He lives in
Brighton, England, with his wife, illustrator Shirley Willis, and
their son Jonathan.

For more information on *The twelve labors of Hercules*
use FactHound to track down Web sites related to this book.

1. Go to *www.facthound.com*
2. Type in a search word related to this
   book or this book ID: 140480904X.
3. Click on the *Fetch It* button.

Your trusty FactHound will fetch the best Web sites for you!

Twelve Labors of Hercules

Table of Contents

The World of Ancient Mythology 4
Introduction .5
The Nemean Lion 6
The Hydra of Lerna 8
The Ceryneian Deer 10
The Erymanthian Boar 12
The Stables of King Augeas 14
The Stymphalian Birds 16
The Cretan Bull 18

The Horses of King Diomedes 20
The Girdle of Hippolyte 22
The Cattle of Geryon 24
The Golden Apples of the Hesperides 26
Keeper of the Underworld 28

Glossary 30
Who's Who 31
Index 32

The World of Ancient Mythology

The ancient Greek civilization was one of the greatest the world has witnessed. It spanned nearly 2,000 years, until it was eventually overwhelmed by the Roman Empire in the second century B.C. At its height, the ancient Greek world extended far beyond what we know as modern Greece.

We owe much to the ancient Greeks. They were great scientists, mathematicians, dramatists, and philosophers. They were also brilliant storytellers. Many of the tales they told were in the form of poetry, often thousands of lines long. The Greeks wrote poems about all kinds of human experiences—love, friendship, war, revenge, history, and even simple everyday activities. The most famous of the poems that have passed down to us are the epic tales of courage and warfare, where brave heroes struggle and suffer against great odds.

A map showing the ancient Greek mainland, surrounding islands, and neighboring lands

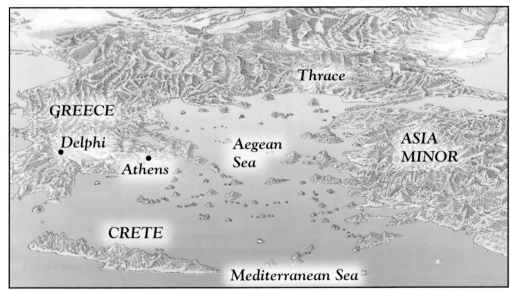

What is incredible is that until the eighth century B.C., the Greeks had no recognized form of writing. All of their stories, lengthy as they were, were handed down from generation to generation by word of mouth. The people who passed on these tales were often professional storytellers, who would perform to music in town squares or public theaters. Often several versions of the same myth existed, depending on who told it and when. What follows is one version of the adventures of Hercules.

If you need help with any of the names, go to the pronunciation guide on page 31.

Introduction

Gather round and hear my story. I will tell you all of the greatest hero the world has ever seen. Of whom am I speaking? Why, Hercules of course! Storytellers of old say that he was the son of a beautiful woman called Alcmene and the king of the gods, Zeus. However, just because his father was a god, it didn't mean that Hercules had an easy life. Zeus's wife, Hera, made sure of that. She was angry that Zeus had fathered a child with a mortal woman, and she despised Hercules. In revenge, she cast a spell on Hercules, which made him kill his wife and children. When Hercules realized the terrible crime he had committed, he asked the famous Oracle at Delphi how he could pay for his dreadful crime. He was told to travel to the kingdom of Mycenae and visit King Eurystheus. Only by obeying the king's every command would Hercules ever be forgiven for killing his family.

I am the storyteller. Lend me your ears!

The Nemean Lion

King Eurystheus was pleased to have a new servant to perform his every wish. For fun, he decided to give Hercules 12 impossible labors, or tasks, and looked forward to seeing the brave young man fail. The first of these was to kill a ferocious lion in the land of Nemea. This fearsome creature had been devouring local people and terrorizing the land. It lived in a deep cave with two entrances, so it always had an escape route. Its skin was so thick that no sword could pierce it. Hercules soon found out that arrows were useless as well. He fired one after another, but they all bounced off harmlessly. So the hero changed his tactics. Hercules blocked off one of the entrances to the lion's den with a huge boulder. Then he chased the beast inside. In this way, he cornered the lion and wrestled it with his bare hands. After a great contest, Hercules strangled the savage beast.

Eurystheus and his jar

When Hercules returned to Eurystheus's kingdom with the dead lion, the king was so terrified by the sight of the beast that he hid in a *pithos*, a large jar made for storing food.

Ask the storyteller

What happened to the lion?

Not wanting to waste his prize, Hercules skinned the dead lion and wore its pelt over his body.

The Hydra of Lerna

King Eurystheus was embarrassed when he eventually emerged from his jar. He decided to give Hercules an even more difficult second task—to kill the Hydra. You will have to stretch your minds to imagine this terrible monster. It had the body of a dragon and nine heads, each with a ravenous mouth lined with sharp teeth. To accomplish his task, Hercules had to travel to the land of Lerna, where the Hydra lived in a swamp.

Facing one enemy was hard enough, but this was like facing nine at the same time. Hercules first tried to chop off the Hydra's heads, but each time he chopped one down, two more grew to replace it. With his enemy multiplying, Hercules came up with a solution. Every time he cut through one of the Hydra's necks, his companion Iolas would hold a lighted torch to the wound to stop a new head from appearing. In this way the Hydra was finally vanquished.

The Poisoned arrows

As the Hydra lay dead, Hercules dipped his arrow tips in the creature's blood, which made them deadly poisonous.

Ask the storyteller

Who was Iolas?

Iolas was the son of Hercules's half-brother Iphicles. As well as helping Hercules with his labors, he was said to drive Hercules's chariot for him.

Quick, Iolas! I think I'm seeing double!

The Ceryneian Deer

Seeing that Hercules had no problems killing creatures, King Eurystheus next sent the hero to capture a magical deer in the land of Ceryneia. This creature was sacred to the goddess Artemis, so it would be a great crime if Hercules were to kill it. The animal had golden antlers and hooves of bronze, and people say it could run as fast as the wind. Whether this is quite true or not, Hercules chased the deer for a whole year without stopping. In the land of Arcadia, he finally was able to immobilize it. He fired an arrow at it, being sure not to kill it. Then he hoisted the beautiful creature onto his broad shoulders and carried his catch back to King Eurystheus. The king demanded that Hercules dedicate the deer to the goddess Artemis at her temple.

A squabble with a god

When Hercules was carrying the deer back to Eurystheus, he met the god Apollo on the way. Apollo tried to take the creature from Hercules, saying that Hercules was trying to kill the sacred animal. However, Hercules managed to explain his actions, and Apollo let him go on his way.

11

The Erymanthian Boar

As his fourth labor, Hercules was sent to capture a ferocious boar, a kind of wild pig, which lived on Mount Erymanthus. This huge creature had long tusks coming from its mouth and a terrible temper. For years it had terrorized the local farmers, destroying their crops and goring them to death.

Hercules forced the animal into the open by shouting threats and throwing his spear, eventually chasing it to the very top of the mountain, where deep snow lay. The boar, now exhausted after the long chase, became stuck in a large snowdrift, and Hercules managed to snare it in a net. He then dragged it all the way back to Mycenae. He didn't get as far as King Eurystheus's palace, however. He just dropped the tied-up boar in the city's marketplace and went to join another hero, Jason, on his ship, the *Argo*.

A battle with the centaurs

Centaurs were creatures that were part horse, part man. On his way to do battle with the boar, Hercules stopped for a drink with a famous centaur called Pholus. This made the other centaurs jealous because they wanted wine, too. They tried to kill Hercules, but he drove them off with flaming logs.

Come on, you fat pig!

Ask the storyteller

What happened to Pholus?

While Hercules was dealing with the angry centaurs, Pholus picked up the hero's bow and arrows to help. Unfortunately, one of the poisoned arrows fell on the centaur's foot and killed him.

The Stables of King Augeas

Hercules had proved that he was both brave and strong, but his next task would require his wits as well. He had to clean out the stables of the king of Elis, called Augeas. This king had more animals than anyone else in Greece, including goats, sheep, horses, and cows. They were all kept together in a stable that had not been cleaned for 30 years. You can imagine the mess! Even so, Hercules was told to complete the task in a single day!

He tackled the problem using his brain more than his brawn. He knocked two holes in opposite ends of the stables. Then, with the help of Iolas, he diverted two nearby rivers, Alpheus and Peneus, so that they flowed through the first hole and washed all the mess out through the second. Hercules managed to clean the colossal mess without so much as dirtying his hands.

Augeas breaks the deal

King Augeas had promised that if Hercules was successful, he could keep one-tenth of the animals for himself. However, when Hercules came to claim his payment, the king refused to give him anything and said that he had never made such a bargain.

Ask the storyteller

Did Hercules leave without a fight?

King Augeas should have thought twice before swindling Hercules. The hero kicked Augeas out of power and placed Augeas's son, Phyleus, on the throne instead.

A job well done, Iolas. You did remember to take out the animals, didn't you?

The Stymphalian Birds

Hercules's sixth labor took him to northern Greece and the land of Stymphalus. Here, above a marsh, lived a flock of birds you'd never want to come across. They were giant winged creatures with bronze beaks and razor-sharp talons. Not surprisingly, they were sacred to the god of war and weapons, Ares, and a terror to the people who farmed in the area. When Hercules arrived, he could not get close to them because he feared treading in the marsh and drowning. Nor could he easily kill them with his arrows. They cowered in the tall trees above or the long marsh grasses below. With a little help from the gods, he found the answer. Using a magical rattle called a *krotala*, he scared the birds out of their hiding places. Then, as they flew away, he quickly shot them down one by one, filling the sky with feathers. At last, the curse of Stymphalus was lifted.

Man-eaters...

...or nuisances?

Some stories say that the birds were flesh-eaters, which carried off children and animals. Others say that they were just a menace, poisoning crops with their droppings. Either way, the people who lived nearby were happy to be rid of them.

PLOP

Ask the storyteller

Where did Hercules get the rattle?

The *krotala* was made by Hephaestus, the god of blacksmiths, who was rumored to be very ugly. He gave the rattle to the goddess Athena, who passed it on to Hercules.

The Cretan Bull

Hercules's seventh labor took him to the island of Crete to capture a famous bull that lived there. The animal was sacred to the god Poseidon and had an interesting history. A man called Minos had wanted to prove to the people of Crete that he was the rightful king, so he asked the gods to send him a miracle that would convince the citizens. Poseidon heard the prayer and made the bull appear out of the sea, much to the astonishment of the Cretans. Minos was supposed to sacrifice the beautiful animal in return. Instead, he kept the magnificent creature for himself. His fate is another story. What we need to know is that Hercules wrestled the bull until he tired it out, then he brought it to King Eurystheus.

The Minotaur

To punish King Minos for not sacrificing the bull, Poseidon made Minos's wife, Pasiphae, fall in love with the creature. To Minos's shame, Pasiphae gave birth to a child called the Minotaur. The Minotaur was half-man, half-bull and ate human flesh! Minos imprisoned this creature in a maze called the Labyrinth, where it was eventually killed by another hero, Theseus.

Ask the storyteller

What happened to the bull?

When Hercules brought the animal before Eurystheus, the king ordered that it be freed. The bull ran amok and ended up in the Plain of Marathon (near Athens), where another hero, Theseus, captured it and sacrificed it to the god Apollo.

Be careful with my pet! He's used to better treatment.

19

The Horses of King Diomedes

By now, Eurystheus was becoming tired of Hercules's successes. This time, he sent him on a particularly dangerous mission, hoping if Hercules returned, at least a few limbs would be missing. So Hercules traveled over the sea to Thrace, where a king named Diomedes ruled over a tribe called the Bistones. Hercules's orders were to capture the four mares that pulled Diomedes's chariot. The problem was that the horses liked the taste of human flesh and would devour anyone who came near them. People say King Diomedes kept them under control by feeding them his unsuspecting guests!

With the help of his friend Abderus, Hercules overcame the grooms who looked after the savage beasts. The hero drove the mares toward the sea where his boat awaited. However, Diomedes and the Bistones caught up with Hercules, and Hercules had to fight them off. Eventually, Hercules escaped with his prize.

Dragged to death

While Hercules dealt with the Bistones, he put his friend Abderus in charge of the mares. Unfortunately, they were too powerful for Abderus to handle, and he was pulled along the ground until he died.

What happened to King Diomedes?

Diomedes came to an unhappy end. Hercules fed the former master to his hungry horses. This magically made them tame and easy to control.

It'll be feeding time soon, Diomedes!

21

The Girdle of Hippolyte

Hercules's next task was of a different kind. By the Aegean Sea lived a band of fierce women called the Amazons. Even the bravest of men thought twice about facing them in battle. Eurystheus ordered Hercules to fetch the girdle, a type of belt, worn by their queen, Hippolyte. This was a belt used to hold her sword and spear, and she would not give it up without a fight. Once again Hercules set sail with a small band of men, determined to accomplish the task.

When Hercules first met Hippolyte, though, she didn't resist his wishes. In fact, she fell instantly in love with him and offered the girdle of her own free will. However, Hercules's old enemy, the goddess Hera, stirred up hatred against him among the other Amazons. In the end, he and his men had to fight a bloody battle. To his regret, Hercules ended up accidentally killing Hippolyte with a stray arrow.

Warrior women

The Amazons hated men. They killed almost all of their male children at birth and made the rest slaves. The girls were raised to be soldiers. Amazon women were especially famous for their prowess on horseback.

Ask the storyteller

Why did Eurystheus want the girdle?

He didn't want it for himself. The king's daughter, Admete, had asked for the girdle as a gift. Eurystheus thought he may as well use Hercules to get it.

The Cattle of Geryon

Hercules's next labor took him to the other side of the known world, to the land of Eurythia. His task was to steal the cattle of Geryon, a giant with three heads, three bodies, and six legs and arms. Some say he was the strongest person who ever lived. Geryon also loved his animals dearly, who were themselves strong, magical beasts.

Geryon's herd was guarded by a shepherd called Eurytion and a snarling, two-headed dog called Orthrus. Hercules first killed these two with his club, before turning to the problem of Geryon himself. It was a very difficult fight because the deformed giant could look in all directions at the same time. However, Hercules devised a way to kill him with a single arrow that pierced all three bodies through their one heart.

The pillars of Hercules

To make his way to Eurythia, Hercules had to part the lands we now know as Africa and Europe. Once the passage was created, Hercules reinforced it with two huge pillars on either side. The pillars would keep the passage open for his return journey.

Ask the storyteller

How did Hercules take the cattle back?

As a reward for his hard work, the sun god, Helios, gave Hercules a great golden bowl in which to cross the sea. It was a rough ride, but he got home in the end.

The Golden Apples of the Hesperides

For Hercules's 11th labor, he had to fetch the golden apples from a sacred garden at the ends of the Earth. The orchard was tended by the Hesperides, nymphs who were daughters of the Titan Atlas. It was also guarded by a terrible, two-headed serpent called Ladon. Hercules had no idea how he would complete the task, but on his way there, he came across some unexpected help. He found a man called Prometheus, who was being punished by the gods because he had stolen from them. Hercules freed him, and in return Prometheus told the hero to seek out Atlas, who would go and get the apples for him. Hercules soon found Atlas, but there was a problem. Atlas's job was to hold the world on his shoulders. So, while Atlas went to fetch the apples, the hero had to hold up the globe in his place.

Oh no! Not again!

Prometheus's punishment

Prometheus had stolen the gift of fire from Mount Olympus and given it to mortal men. As a punishment, Zeus had chained him to a cliff, where every day a giant eagle would come down and peck out his liver. Every night the liver grew back, so Prometheus's torture was never-ending.

Keeper of the Underworld

Hercules had now been at his labors for 11 long years. His final duty was by far the most dangerous. King Eurystheus told him to descend to the Underworld, the land of the dead. This was a task that few mortals had managed. On top of that, Hercules would have to bring back the ferocious dog Cerberus, who guarded the dark kingdom. However, Cerberus was no ordinary dog. He had three heads and a coat writhing with poisonous snakes.

Hercules descended into the Underworld through a cavern in a place called Taenarum. He then crossed the River Styx and visited Hades, ruler of the dead, and asked if he could take the dog away. Hades gave him permission, provided he use only his brute strength and no weapons. Hercules succeeded, but when he took the beast before Eurystheus, the king was so scared, he ordered it to be returned immediately.

Rescuing an old friend

While in the Underworld, Hercules freed his friend, the hero Theseus. Theseus and his friend Perithous had been captured trying to free Hades's queen, Persephone. Hades had abducted Persephone from the land of the living.

Ask the storyteller

Is that the end?

With his 12 labors completed, Hercules had fulfilled his debt to Hera. He went on to become the most famous of all Greek heroes, celebrated in art and poetry for centuries to come.

Glossary

Abducted Kidnapped.

Amazons A race of warrior women who lived in Asia.

Amok In a wild way.

Centaur A mythical creature that was half-man, half-horse.

Girdle A type of belt.

Groom Someone who looks after horses.

Immobilize To make something unable to move.

Mortal A being who will die one day, or who can be killed.

Mount Olympus The home of Zeus and other Olympian gods.

Nymph A beautiful young woman related to the gods.

Oracle A person who can tell what will happen in the future.

Pelt The skin of a dead animal.

Prowess Skill or strength.

Ravenous Very hungry.

Sacred When something is respected because it is holy and comes from the gods.

Sacrifice To kill a person or animal as a gift to a god.

Temple A place of worship. Most gods had temples built in their honor.

Titan One of a race of giant gods overthrown by Zeus.

Underworld The place in Greek mythology where people go after they die.

Vanquished Overcome by force.

Who's Who

Abderus (ab-DEE-rus) Companion of Hercules.

Admete (ad-MEE-tee) Daughter of Eurystheus.

Alcmene (alk-MEE-nuh) Mother of Hercules.

Apollo (uh-POLL-oh) Greek god of medicine and music.

Ares (AIR-eez) Greek god of war.

Artemis (ARE-tuh-miss) Greek goddess of hunting.

Athena (uh-THEE-nah) Greek goddess of wisdom and war.

Atlas (AT-luss) A Titan; god who held up the world on his shoulders.

Augeas (aw-JEE-ass) A king who owned thousands of animals.

Bistones (bis-TOE-neez) The race ruled by King Diomedes.

Cerberus (SER-ber-us) The dog who guarded the Underworld.

Diomedes (die-oh-MEE-deez) A king who owned four man-eating horses.

Eurystheus (you-RISS-thee-us) The king who ordered Hercules's labors.

Eurytion (you-RIT-ee-on) The shepherd who guarded Geryon's cattle.

Geryon (GEE-ree-on) A three-headed, three-bodied giant.

Hades (HEY-deez) Greek god of the Underworld.

Helios (HEE-lee-oss) Greek sun god.

Hephaestus (hih-FES-tuss) Greek god of blacksmiths.

Hera (HEE-rah) A goddess and wife of Zeus who despised Hercules.

Hercules (HER-cue-leez) The most famous Greek hero.

Hesperides (hess-PE-rid-eez) Nymphs and daughters of Atlas.

Hippolyte (hi-PO-lit-ee) Queen of the Amazons.

Iolas (YO-lass) Companion and nephew of Hercules.

Iphicles (IF-ick-leez) Half-brother of Hercules.

Jason (JAY-sun) A Greek hero who stole a famous golden fleece.

Ladon (LA-don) Two-headed serpent that guarded the golden apples of the Hesperides.

Minos (MINE-oss) King of Crete.

Minotaur (MIN-uh-tore) A creature who was half-man, half-bull.

Orthrus (OR-thruss) The dog belonging to Eurytion.

Pasiphae (PASS-if-ee) Minos's wife and the Minotaur's mother.

Perithous (PE-rith-oos) A Greek hero.

Persephone (per-SEF-on-ee) A goddess abducted by Hades.

Pholus (FOH-luss) A centaur.

Phyleus (FYE-lee-us) King Augeas's son.

Poseidon (poss-EYE-don) Greek god of the sea.

Prometheus (pro-MEE-thee-us) A man who stole the secret of fire from the gods and gave it to mortals.

Theseus (THEE-see-us) A Greek hero.

Zeus (ZOOS) King of the Greek gods.

Index

A

Abderus, 20, 31
Admete, 23, 31
Alcmene, 5, 31
Alpheus, River, 14
Amazons, 22, 30
Apollo, 10, 19, 31
Ares, 16, 31
Argo, 12
arrows, 6, 10
  poisoned, 8, 13
Artemis, 10–11, 31
Athena, 17, 31
Atlas, 26–27, 31
Augeas, King, 14–15, 31

B

birds (of Stymphalus), 16
Bistones, 20, 31
boar (of Erymanthus), 12
bull (Cretan), 18–19

C

centaurs, 12–13, 30, 31
Cerberus, 28, 31

D

deer (of Ceryneia), 10
Diomedes, 20–21, 31

E

eagle, 26
Elis, 14
Erymanthus, Mount, 12
Eurystheus, King, 5, 6, 8, 10, 12,
  18–19, 20, 23, 28, 31
Eurythia, 24
Eurytion, 24, 31

G

Geryon, 24, 31
Girdle (of Hippolyte), 22–23, 30
golden apples, 26

H

Hades, 28, 31
Helios, 25, 31
Hephaestus, 17, 30, 31
Hera, 5, 22, 29, 31
Hesperides, 26, 31
Hippolyte, 22, 31
horses (of Diomedes), 20–21
Hydra, 8

I

Iolas, 8–9, 14, 31
Iphicles, 9, 31

J

Jason, 12, 31

K

krotala, 16–17

L

Labyrinth, 18
Ladon, 26, 31
Lerna, 8
lion (of Nemea), 6–7

M

Marathon, Plain of, 19
Minos, king of Crete, 18, 31
Minotaur, 18, 31
Mycenae, 5, 12

N

nymphs, 26, 30

O

Olympus, Mount, 26, 30
Oracle at Delphi, 5
Orthrus, 24, 31

P

Pasiphae, 18, 31
Peneus, River, 14
Perithous, 28, 31
Persephone, 28, 31
Pholus, 12–13, 31
Phyleus, 15, 31
pillars (of Hercules), 24
pithos, 6
Poseidon, 18, 31
Prometheus, 26, 31

S

stables (of King Augeas), 14
Stymphalus, 16
Styx, River, 28

T

Taenarum, 28
Theseus, 18–19, 28, 31
Thrace, 20
Titan, 26, 30, 31

U

Underworld, 28, 30, 31

Z

Zeus, 5, 26–27, 30, 31